Haunting

by

Ray Alexander

3RD April 1996.
Bought from Author in York.

© Ray Alexander 1995
All rights reserved by copyright owner

Published by Quacks Books
Petergate, York YO1 2HT
in association with
INTER-media, 15 Hawthorn Terrace, New Earswick,
York, YO3 4 BL

British Library Cataloguing Publication Data
Alexander, Ray 1995
Haunting York
Great Britain

ISBN NUMBER 0 948333 53 7

Price £3.50

vi, 42pp

Printed by Quacks Printers, 7 Grape Lane, York, YO1 2HU

Acknowledgements

The definitive study of the hauntings of York is, in my opinion, John V. Mitchell's *Ghosts of an Ancient City* which was first published in 1973. I acknowledge with thanks my debt to him for his book which was the source volume for all the stories retold here, with the obvious exception of those which have occurred more recently.

The other volumes that I have used as reference are included in a bibliography and I thank their authors. There may be other works that I have read over the years which have had an influence on me but have not been mentioned here, to their authors I also give my thanks.

My gratitude is also due to Mark S. Graham who invited me to join The Original Ghost Walk of York as a guide, enabling me to tell these stories in person in the streets of York.

And Lottie Alexander for her help, advice and attention to detail.

Introduction

Pervading the City of York is a character and atmosphere that comes from over two thousand years of human habitation. Overwhelmingly, there seems to be the presence of all those generations of inhabitants whose labour and love for the city have made it what it is today. It's as if they want to take you back to a time when the pace of life was dictated by the rising and the setting of the sun and when a person on foot travelled fast enough for the needs of the day. So even now, someone rushing through the City seems to be moving with indecent haste.

Perhaps some of those ancient citizens do manage to make contact with us in the form of the ghosts for which the city has become famous.

Popular interest in the ghosts of York started when John Mitchell, a teacher at St Olave's School, told stories to his pupils as a way of interesting them in the history of the City. In 1973 he published *Ghosts of an Ancient City,* and this was followed by guided walks of the haunted sites which have developed over the years into a popular and characteristic attraction for residents of York and its visitors. The guided tour that his book initiated still runs today as The Original Ghost Walk.

In a Tyne-Tees Television programme about ghosts, John Mitchell said, "Ghosts are strange creatures, I have a love-hate relationship with them. When you go looking for them they're never there." This seems to be the case with most of the instances included in this book; they occurred to people who weren't looking for ghosts, had little or no interest in them and probably didn't believe in them anyway.

It is intriguing that, despite the lack of scientific evidence for the existence of ghosts, they seem to have held the human race in a state of fascination for centuries. Whether the stories are true or invented doesn't seem to matter: they hold our attention and grip our minds. The inquisitive have always been enthralled by the large amount of fiction on the subject; but it is the stories told by people of their own experiences that fascinate believers and sceptics alike.

Believers add these events to the store of experience and theory that they use to prove their case. Sceptics argue that they only increase the large number of questions that still remain to be answered. Overall, there are too many kinds of hauntings to be able to find one simple explanation for them all, but by grouping together common themes and occurrences from individual hauntings it has been possible to develop a number of theories.

Powerful human bonds, it has been suggested, have caused people to see ghosts of close friends or relatives near to the moment of death, sometimes when they were countries or even continents apart. The absence of a priest's blessing at the time of death, or being buried without a religious ceremony, may have caused spirits to remain trapped on earth as ghosts. The changing of a location, either by building on it or altering the building that is there, seems to be able to start or stop a haunting. A need to interact with the living seems to have created "lost souls" trying to attract attention to themselves because of some great injustice during life; perhaps they are trying to appeal to the living to right the wrong. Similar to this but more malignant, is the instance of people who have been evil or antisocial in life and appear to continue to be so after death, making life uncomfortable for the living. Sometimes, a desire to keep a grip on their place on earth may have enabled owners of properties, housekeepers or people with a strong emotional commitment to a place, to stay long after death to act as guardians.

Perhaps the most evocative theory suggests that great human emotion, trauma, passion, even love, can imprint itself into the fabric of the place where it occurs. It remains there until it is played back in the mind of someone with a similar psyche to the person who had the original experience, causing them to superimpose images of the events of the past onto the locations that they are actually seeing at the time. This is probably the most scientific theory of them all, yet it still relies on some unexplained activity of the brain to make it work.

Over the years scientists and sceptics have investigated hauntings in an attempt to provide definitive proof for or against the existence of ghosts. In most cases logical explanations have emerged to show that natural rather than supernatural forces were at work. Sometimes, however, there is a case that they can't explain. When this occurs there is always one question remaining - *if it can't be proved to be false, is it possible that it can be true?*

Most of the stories in this book are well documented in other places and have passed into folk lore. But because they are events that have happened to people, they have usually been told in the style of a newspaper report which tends to make them bland and shallow by comparison with fictional ghost stories. For that reason I have taken some liberties in telling these stories by taking the basic facts and weaving them into a tale in the fashion of traditional storytelling.

I hope that this will enhance your enjoyment of the stories and that you will find them haunting...

... Micklegate Bar

History records the deeds of the great, the extremely good and the extremely bad, but tends, in general, to ignore everyone else. For the vast majority of people just their births, marriages and deaths are all that are usually recorded for those who come after. For centuries people shaped the world in which we now live, but their legacy rarely contains a sign to identify their contribution. A desire to discover the mark left on the planet by our ancestors has encouraged some people to research into the history of their families; searches that have brought people from all over the world to York, where their forebears may have spent some time and perhaps left an imprint in the history of the City.

The search for such an imprint was the reason that one woman came to York some years ago. She was aware that many generations of her family had lived in the City and that some of their activities may have been recorded. Taking a break from her work she spent a day leisurely wandering around the streets enjoying the sights and sounds and atmosphere of that very ancient settlement. Then as evening drew on she started to make her way towards her hotel near the race course and as she crossed Ouse Bridge, the image of how it had been a few centuries ago slipped into her mind. The clutter of buildings; shops, houses, a school, a chapel, toll booths and two prisons. She could imagine the bustle of shoppers and travellers, horses and carts all using the only bridge across the River Ouse. Children scampered after a dog ignoring the vagrant who begged a coin. She had nearly crossed the bridge and was near to where one of the prisons had once stood, when a feeling of uneasiness crept into her reverie. It was a strange sensation of sadness; a new emotion to her and one that she couldn't quite properly define. With a sudden sense of urgency she walked off the bridge and continued on her way up Micklegate with echoes of the feeling still tormenting her.

As she reached the brow of the hill and approached Micklegate Bar, the sadness was replaced by an uncanny sense of fascination. She found herself being drawn towards the Bar. Slowly she made her way to one side of it and climbed the steps onto the wall. Intrigued by this new sensation she walked towards Toft Green, the wall became a narrow ribbon that she had to follow. It stretched ahead of her with the castellated parapet

to her left and a sheer drop of about six feet to the steeply sloping ramparts on her right. The wall seemed to draw her along its length almost against her will, as if some memory, deep in her subconscious was insisting that she should go on.

At Tofts Tower she paused for a while to admire the view. Outside the wall was the railway station, but she found it easy to imagine what it must have been like when it was just an expanse of fields with the Ouse away in the distance. Turning to look inwards she found the sight of the nearby modern buildings uninspiring, alleviated only by the beauty of the Minster on the horizon. She walked on. Barely a hundred yards from the tower she was suddenly overtaken by a sensation of intense terror. The feeling was so strong that she thought she was going to faint, anxiously she looked around for help but she was completely alone.

The wall, in one direction led past the station towards Lendal Bridge and although it was a means of escape, it seemed a million miles away. In the other direction was Micklegate Bar and yet, somehow, she feared to return to it. Her head was spinning and everything looked different, the buildings and station had gone and in their place were open spaces, a few buildings that looked like a monastery and, dotted about the landscape, people who seemed to be miles away, as if at the end of a tunnel. None of them looked her way as the intensity of her distress increased.

Overwhelmed by the sensation and terrified by a feeling of helplessness, her knees grew weak and her glance fell to the pavement where she saw, not far away, the lower half of a monk and before she could react, heard a reassuring male voice.

"Don't be afraid. Follow me."

"Thank God," she whispered and followed the man back the way she had come. Unwilling to lift her eyes from the pavement, she kept them fixed firmly on the monk as she tried to ignore the changed landscape around her. Mesmerised by the easy rhythm of his gait she followed, feeling her confidence return as they approached the Bar. Later she realised that at no time did she looked at his face.

When they reached the steps leading back to the street, the man stood to one side allowing her to descend from the wall. On the top step she turned round to thank him for his kindness. It had only taken a few seconds for her to walk past him and turn round, yet in that time he had gone. Her vision had cleared, the buildings returned, city life was back to normal but the wall was completely deserted. For a long way in each direction there was nobody.

Unsteadily she made her way back to the street.

Unable to explain the experience nor to understand the meaning of it, she put it away in her memory as one of the strange and interesting things that can happen to you in a city as old as York and she continued with her research into her ancestry.

She also widened her researches into the history of the city, concentrating in particular on the area around Micklegate Bar. At one time it was the royal entrance to York where, traditionally, visiting monarchs were met by the Lord Mayor and civic dignitaries before being escorted into the city. It was also the place where the severed heads of traitors were displayed on wooden pikes as a warning to others. One head that was displayed there was that of Richard, Duke of York in 1460. She remembered the lines from Shakespeare's Henry VI part 3, where Queen Margaret orders,

> Off with his head, and set it on York gates;
> So York may overlook the town of York.

A more surprising discovery was that she was related to a man who had fought in the Battle of Boroughbridge in 1322; he had been captured, was publicly executed and his head, also, was piked over Micklegate Bar. Before it was piked the head would have lain for several days in one of the toll booths in the prisons on Ouse bridge. This, she thought, might possibly offer an explanation for the strange emotions she had felt on the bridge and the wall. But it still left a mystery concerning the identity of the monk who had led her to safety.

A map of mediaeval York provided an answer. Inside the wall, close to the point where she had almost fainted, there was once an order of Dominican Friars. They wore black habits, vowed to lead a life of simplicity and poverty and were noted for carrying out acts of charity for prisoners who were condemned to death.

Her helper, she believed, had been a ghost.

The ghost of a monk, who in life, had lived in that part of the city and may have given comfort to her relative when he was condemned to death many centuries before.

... Theatres

In the search to find rational explanations for the appearance of ghosts, a number of theories have emerged and one is that they simply want to draw attention to themselves. As if to prove this, some ghosts have chosen what might be considered the ideal place for it, the theatre. Both of the principal theatres in York can claim to have one or two performers from the supernatural world.

In a narrow street leading to the River Ouse stands The Grand Opera House. Until recently it was a bingo hall known as the SS Empire and every day the cleaners would make their way through the building removing the debris of the previous night's entertainment in preparation for the next. One of them was Mrs Laura Scott, who, like everyone who worked there, had been told that there was a ghost of a woman in grey in the building. But Laura had just laughed. "Don't be so stupid," she told them, more interested in getting on with her work than in spending time fantasising about ghosts.

For two centuries, generations of her family had lived at the riverside working in shipbuilding, so Laura knew the way of life of the area and was familiar with all its stories and folk tales. With another woman she had the regular job of cleaning the gallery and although she didn't believe the place was haunted, she always thought that it looked weird when lit by only the working lights. There was harsh light in some places that created deep shadows in others. A world of evil could hide in those shadows if your mind would only let it. But Laura's wouldn't, she had a no-nonsense attitude to life.

Everything followed its usual pattern until one day her friend failed to come to work. With no one spare to replace her, Laura made her way up the stairs to the top of the theatre knowing that she would have twice as much to do that day. The other women said they would try to find time to give her a hand, but initially Laura was on her own. Ignoring the eerie look of the gallery, she buckled down to the job.

She had been up there some time and was well on with the work when she noticed that the atmosphere had changed, it had suddenly become icy cold. Laura started to shiver and stood up straight. Uneasily, she looked around. The vast area of empty seats bathed in the eerie-looking light sent a quiver of fear down her spine, but she was relieved to find that

she was still alone. Shaking off the uncomfortable feeling she returned to her work, then something made her look up again. Now she wasn't alone.

To her amazement, a figure was approaching her. One of her workmates, she thought, dressed up and trying to frighten her. But it didn't look right.

This wasn't a human being - it appeared to be made of cobwebs.

It was like a fog coming towards her, there was no face nor any details that she could identify. The figure stayed on the gallery for some time, always some distance from her, but a definite presence. For a while Laura was unable to move, but when the figure came no closer to her, she tried to get on with her work and put it to the back of her mind, determined that she wouldn't be driven away. As she worked she became aware that the temperature was slowly returning to normal and the next time she looked up the figure had gone. The harsh lights and deep shadows were still there, but there was no harm lurking in them.

Everyday after that, Laura found herself looking for the figure and was, perhaps, just a little relieved when it never appeared again. Maybe that was because the circumstances were never the same again or, perhaps, being ignored is as bad for ghosts as it is for actors.

Across the city and close to the Minster stands the Theatre Royal. It was built in 1744 on the site of St Leonard's Hospital and part of the hospital's vaulted cloister still remains in the present building. One of the ghosts is believed to have its origins in that earlier time. Another, hard to identify because of the lack of contemporary records, is the ghost of an actor who had once performed on the stage.

Pride and a fiery disposition are a dangerous combination in anyone, but added to the artistic temperament of an actor, the mixture can be lethal. For one actor it also led to a premature death and an unscheduled posthumous appearance. For reasons long lost in the mists of time, the actor was involved in an argument with an ordinary citizen of York which ended when he was challenged to a duel. Honour, pride and the conviction that he could not loose led him to accept the challenge. In his acting career he had fought any number of duels on stage and like most members of his profession, was an excellent swordsman. A crowd assembled in Blake Street to watch the duel and with all the dignity of a great actor he took up his position on the field of battle, barely hours before he was due to appear on stage. He greeted his opponent with the assurance of one who had faced more able enemies before and who had always won. His eyes glinted as he flashed a few practice strokes in the air, then with a theatrical flourish, rehearsed the stab that would bring down his opponent. The crowd cheered and applauded in excited anticipation. The man he was to fight stood impassive and a little bewildered; this was a new experience to him and the antics of the actor left him wondering what to do. He did nothing.

The duel began with the actor putting up a brave show as he had done in many of the fictional battles he had fought on stage. In his mind he had planned and plotted the fight with lots of exciting moves, a moment or two of danger when it would look as though he was about to loose and then, in a final desperate effort he would rise from the brink of defeat and in a thrilling climax, strike his opponent down and leave the field of battle in triumph, cloaked only by the modesty of a true hero.

But Fate had written a different line.
The actor danced around the man he had slighted, swinging his sword wildly. It soon became apparent that his opponent wasn't an actor and didn't know the rituals of the theatre nor what was expected of him. Bewildered, he stood and watched the antics of the actor as he entertained the crowd. Finally, out of his depth and angered by their jeers, he stepped aside to avoid one of the actor's flourishes, bent his knees and slid his sword

beneath the actor's arm.

That afternoon the player took his final curtain call.

His shocked fellow actors were in the street to witness his dying scene, which they all felt, he carried off rather well; as Shakespeare had put it,

> Nothing in his life
> Became him like the leaving of it: he died
> As one that had been studied in his death,
> To throw away the dearest thing he ow'd,
> As 'twere a careless trifle.

A few hours later, with little ceremony for the late and barely lamented actor, the play went ahead. News of the duel had flashed around the city and the house was packed to overflowing with the air full of expectancy for humour and an impending disaster as the understudy took the stage. Just as the cue came for his first entrance, all the players assembled in the wings.

To their amazement they also saw their dead colleague staggering about the side of the stage, as if attempting to make his entrance. He looked as they had seen him last, not in his costume, but in clothes dripping with blood. He appeared to be tormented and in great pain and reached an arm towards the stage as if appealing for it to draw him before his audience. The stage ignored his appeal. The cue came and, after a moment of hesitation, the understudy walked on. Then, as all the attention was diverted towards the action on stage, the old actor slowly faded away.

After the performance the company gathered in the ale house and discussed the unusual turn of events that day. Much of the conversation centred on the unexpected arrival in the wings of their dead friend. At first they thought that he wasn't dead at all, then that he had risen from the dead and, finally, concluded that the power of his spirit, determined not to let down his audience had probably caused him to try to make his entrance as usual. But seeing his understudy well in command of the situation, his spirit made its final exit, hopefully, to rest in peace.

The other, much older and more frequently seen ghost has been called the Grey Lady. The appearance of a little nun wearing a grey habit and a white coif in the circle has been witnessed by several actors. On one occasion the entire company of a production of *Dear Octopus* including, Miss Evelyn Laye, saw the misty figure in the dress circle watching their rehearsal. The production was a triumph, which led to the belief that seeing the Grey Lady was a sign of a good run. Nowadays actors may be tempted to glimpse into the gloom of the auditorium for a sight of the figure that will herald a success.

But if the Grey Lady is taken to be an omen of good tidings, her story is one of misery and tragedy and starts long before the theatre was built. The Theatre Royal stands on the vaulted cloisters of St Leonard's Hospital which once occupied the site. The hospital was administered by a religious order which laid down strict rules of behaviour for its followers. They were forbidden to leave the hospital without permission and if they did, they had to go in pairs. They could eat only at set meal times and not at all outside the hospital.

At one time a Sister was believed to have broken the most important rule of all, she had a friendship with a man from outside the religious community. Under traditional rights granted by Henry I, the hospital was able to "hold court and judge;" she was tried in private and condemned to be locked away from all living things. In a quiet corner of a building not far from the Minster, she was put into a small room that had no windows, the door was shut and locked and then sealed up.

Distressed and alone, she was left to die.

The Theatre Royal now stands on the site where this vile punishment was performed and its exact location is believed to be one of the dressing rooms behind the dress circle. Some actors have sensed a strange atmosphere there which has disturbed them so much that they asked for another room; they may have been experiencing sympathy with the agony of her ordeal. But others have requested to use it because they felt there was a friendly spirit present.

It is also believed that she is that lonely figure sometimes seen in the auditorium watching the rehearsals. In what was once the place of her torment, she now watches the present day inhabitants bringing pleasure and joy to others.

...Pubs

The cosy surroundings created by the ancient interiors of York's pubs might easily lull the visitor into a feeling of ease and well-being. A very dangerous state; because it is in such conditions that ghosts are most often experienced.

As travellers make their way through the narrow streets that lead away from the Minster, they may be intrigued by their ancient names, Bedern (Bedaere - the place of prayer), Spen Lane (at one time Ispingail - the lane overgrown with Aspens), Aldwark (old Roman workings) and Peaseholme Green (the islet or place by the water where peas are grown). Arriving in Peaseholme Green their attention will be drawn to the Black Swan Inn with its echoes of an age long since past. Built in the seventeenth century, it has many features from an earlier age and an history which dates back to the fifteenth century.

Entering the inn through the old oak door, customers move down the long passage that leads to the main bar with its oak beams, large inglenook fireplace, and warm atmosphere. It also has some regulars who never buy a drink. One of them is a young woman who has been seen standing and staring out of the window. She seems out of place in the modern pub setting, as though the the room she is in is not the one that exists now. She always has her back to the room and no one has ever seen her face, the way she stands suggests that she is pensive or sad; her clothes are those of the turn of the century and it looks as if she is waiting for someone. During the winter months, she can be seen standing by the inglenook staring into the fire, watching the flames as they flicker and jump up the chimney. Still she has her back to the room and after a while she gives up her lonely wait, gently fading into the atmosphere.

On other occassions another non-drinking visitor is seen, this time a man who also wears clothes from the same period. Although they have never appeared at the same time, it is thought that the two might be connected. The man sits in the chair in the inglenook beside the fire, but the chair somehow appears to be different from the one that is actually there. On his lap there is an object that might be a gift, a bunch of flowers or something in a colourful wrapping - nobody is quite sure. He stares into the room but sees no one, after waiting for only a short time he gives up; then he fades away.

One thing that the visitor to The Black Swan will notice is that no matter how busy the pub is, that chair will be one of the last to be taken. And very rarely will one of the regulars ever sit there.

The identities of these people and the reason they appear is a mystery, it has been suggested that they may have been lovers who were forbidden to see each other. An illicit meeting was arranged but an accident may have caused them to miss each other, possibly with fatal consequences. Now it seems they are locked in an eternal time warp, destined never to meet again but to appear from time to time and wait a few moments before fading once more into oblivion.

Generally speaking, those in search of ghosts rarely see them; but sometimes ghost hunters can get more than they bargained for. Just before Christmas, 1990, the landlord received a letter of thanks from two of his guests, Carl and Vicki from Anchorage, Alaska, together with an account of an incident they had experienced while staying at the inn that summer.

They had heard that the pub was haunted and they wanted to spend the night there. They arrived on 16th June, 1990 and were delighted with the room they were given. Wandering the ancient and narrow streets of the city that afternoon, heightened their anticipation for a night to be spent in an haunted inn. By ten o'clock they had retired to their room. The door was locked and bolted.

At half past two they were woken by footsteps immediately outside their door. A second later the footsteps were inside the room and moving towards the bed, stopping just a short distance from it. Hanging in the air was a presence, but they could see nothing and there wasn't a sound in the house. Carl and Vicki lay still and silent; looking and listening. After a while the presence in the room seemed to disappear and slowly Vicki drifted off into peaceful sleep, but Carl remained awake with his attention focused on the room.

Time drifted by, he was not sure how long he lay there before he became aware of a glimmer of light over his head. He thought it was the product of an over active mind, so he immediately looked to another part of the room but saw nothing. Returning his gaze to the place where he saw the glimmer he found that it was still there, but now it was growing and slowly starting to take on form. At first it was little more than a hazy image, then slowly features became clear and he was able to see the face of a man. Now he wished it was his imagination because he would be able to shut it out of his mind.

The head appeared to be hanging in the air a little above him. It was bald on top with long, thin grey hair at the sides, the eyes were open and now he could see, quite clearly the face of a man aged about 50. Carl thought that the face was full of anger, the mouth appeared to be speaking, but no words emerged. Mercifully, it disappeared a short time later and Carl slipped away into sleep.

The next morning Vicki said she slept through Carl's experience, but had dreams about angry people. They had crossed the Atlantic in search of an unusual experience and to spend the night in an haunted hotel, they chose an hotel in York and were not disappointed.

Sometimes alterations to a place or a building have appeared to either start or stop a haunting. Strange events started happening when the old Plumbers' Arms, in Skeldergate was converted into a modern pub and renamed the Cock and Bottle. People, not even in their cups, have witnessed objects moving when no one is near them, locked doors that have mysteriously opened or, more worryingly, locked themselves; pictures that have fallen from walls and lights that have been mysteriously switched on or off. Some people have complained of the sensation of a presence in the room with eyes staring intently at them. On occasions, even on a warm summer's evening, a sudden and chill has run through the bar, freezing drinkers in mid sentence. When attempts to find explanations in terms of

The old Plumber's Arms

trickery, illusion and intoxication have been exhausted and still not provided an answer; one question remains - what has caused it? There appears to be no logical explanation for much of this and, although illogical, many believe that the supernatural may provide the answer.

In the mid 1960's it was decided that the building that had stood in Skeldergate since 1575 needed modernising, the result was a new exterior, leaving many antique internal features intact. It may be these alterations that have disturbed something was lying deep in the history of the building. Something long forgotten and at peace, until now.

In the seventeenth century the house in the grounds of Buckingham House, the home of George Villiers, the second Duke of Buckingham. He was a spendthrift, a drunkard, a gambler and a womaniser and despite being a great favourite of the King, Charles II, he was hated and ridiculed. He was a supporter of the Royalists during the Civil War and went into exile after their defeat. His exploits in France during that time were made famous by Alexandre Dumas in *The Three Musketeers* and his fame was made complete when the Poet Laureate, John Dryden, wrote a verse about him the poem "Absalom and Achitophel" in which he was ridiculed for being a "chemist, fiddler, statesman and buffoon" all in the course of a month. It has been suggested that the rhyme "Georgie Porgie" also applied to Villiers.

The ridicule of his contemporaries seemed to have had little effect on Villiers who used the house on the banks of the Ouse, for some of his more nefarious pleasures, one of which was alchemy. At night, alone in his cottage down by the river, he tried to turn ordinary metals into gold and to brew a potion that would give him eternal life. People feared to go near the place, especially at night, when he was conducting his mysterious experiments. Strangely coloured, flickering lights pierced the night sky and evil-smelling fumes filled the air and clogged the throat. His ambition was to be very rich and live forever, but it was believed that he actually had a more sinister purpose in mind. Some said he was trying to call up the devil, but others thought differently, they were sure that he was the devil.

His unpopularity grew until, deeply in debt and socially disgraced, he was forced to leave York and take up residence in Helmsley Castle. One day while hunting he suffered an accident and was carried to a house in Kirkbymoorside, a chill set in and his life rapidly ebbed away. As he lay dying, he expressed a wish to be buried at York, but, as a member of the aristocracy he had to be taken to Westminster Abbey in London where, in an ironic twist of fate for one who was so notorious in his lifetime, he was laid to rest in an unmarked tomb. So, although London may have his bones, York appears to have his ghost.

The interior of the modern pub still has many of the features of Villiers' old house, but is greatly altered. It is unlikely that he would have approved the alterations, although he might have liked the idea that the house where he enjoyed so much profligate pleasure, was being used today by the drinkers of the City. Perhaps he has even come back to join them.

A figure resembling the description of Villiers, with a broad brimmed hat over long curly hair and a lace stock at his neck has often been seen sitting in the bar; but whenever approached it has faded into the fabric of the building. Sometimes women have complained that they have been touched by unseen hands and have accused their companions who swear their innocence, telling the story of Villiers' and explaining how his ghost behaves in death as he did in life. For some it is an acceptable explanation, but for others it seems that poor old "Georgie Porgie" is being blamed for the activities of his modern day counterparts.

Not a pub, until recently a restaurant known as the Four Seasons, but haunted nonetheless. It is the home of a sad ghost that makes itself known as a presence in the upper part of the house, particularly on the stairs and by lights which are switched on and off or by doors that are opened and closed.

Just recently the manageress was cashing up after the day's business when she heard the sounds of someone crying in the building. She knew that there was no one else there, yet from very close by she could hear the sound of a pittiful sobbing. The realisation that she was alone made her blood run cold. Later she checked in the next door pub where they assured her that nobody there had been crying that evening.

One of the last tasks for the supervisor each night was to write the menu board in chalk ready for the next day, but many times they opened the restaurant in the morning to find that a hand had been rubbed through the writing. The manageress always made it a habit to say good morning to the ghost she called "Marm" as she entered the building, although she wasn't sure whether this was out of respect or fear. These events are minor and do nothing to disturb the peace of the house and are there, it has been suggested, to draw attention to a tragic life lived several centuries ago.

During the seventeenth century, the house was the home of the Buckle family and just before the end of the century Marmaduke was born, but was destined to a miserable and short life. He was crippled and marked as an outcast. Trapped within a deformed body in a society where he had no place he became desparate. He spent his time in the upper rooms of the house, sad and alone, until finally he took his destiny into his own hands.

Into the wall he scratched his name "Marmaduke Buckle", then under it the year, 1715; under that he marked the date of his birth, 1697, under which he drew a line and beneath it added the result of a calculation - his age - 17. When he had finished he took a rope and threw it over the long beam that supports the roof, fixing it firmly so that it wouldn't slip, he tied a loop into the other end. With nothing to live for the seventeen year-old took his life in the room where he had spent most of his life alone. Leaving that poignant memorial:

Marmaduke Buckle
1715
<u>1697</u>
17

... Clifford's Tower

In 1069, for the second time in a year, William the Conqueror returned to York to suppress a rebellion. While he was there his troops threw up an earth mound on the northern bank of the River Ouse and on it he had them build a wooden tower to add to the one they built on the southern bank the previous year. The two became known collectively as York Castle. A little over a century later the castle was burned to the ground during another uprising. It was replaced during the thirteenth century by a stone tower built on the site of William's castle. In 1322, after the battle of Boroughbridge, the corpse of Robert de Clifford was hung there in chains as a public warning and the castle gained a new name, Clifford's Tower.

The tower was built in 1245 but shortly after its completion, amazed and terrified citizens of York saw that its walls had turned red.

They demanded and explanation for it and such experts as they had at the time suggested that there was a fungus in the stone that gave it a red appearance, or maybe a chemical, perhaps an oxide, which when wet, looked red. This failed to satisfy the people of York because they had something on their consciences and an explanation of their own - they said the walls were running with Jewish blood. Nothing could be said to dispel this thought from their minds and it was such a powerful image that they handed it down in the folk lore of the city, so that when the same phenomenon occurred on subsequent occasions, the people of York knew that the stones of the castle were running with the blood of the Jews. The events that are believed to have caused this horrific vision lie deep in the history of the city.

Jews in England during the Norman period were unmercifully persecuted, nowhere less so than in the City of York. The end of 1189 saw the coronation of Richard I, Richard Lion-Heart and within a year he had departed on a crusade. The Jews who had enjoyed the protection of his father, Henry II, now felt exposed and feared for their lives. Poverty was rife and the Jewish community was generally blamed for all the ills of the country. Unable to lead lives as normal citizens, their only recourse was to become money lenders. So the nation that persecuted them and particularly the monarch, depended on them for a supply of wealth. Many foreign wars were fought with Jewish money.

Two leading York Jews, Benedict and Joseph, travelled to London to celebrate the coronation of King Richard. While they were there, anti-Jewish feeling resulted in Benedict being attacked in the streets. They struggled to return to York, but overwhelmed by his injuries, Benedict died in Nottingham. At the same time in York, an elderly Jew called Isaac, was attacked in Coney Street, holy water poured over him and he was forced to eat pork before he was murdered. As if the death of Benedict wasn't enough, in March 1190, rebels broke into his home, stole his valuables, killed his widow and children and set light to the house.

This seems to have been the signal for an attack on the whole Jewish community. Seeking refuge from their persecutors, the Jews fled to the castle where the constable took them in. The persecutors under the leadership of a man called Richard Malebisse and a white-robed monk followed them and laid seige to the castle. Malebisse offered the Jews their freedom if they would hand over all their valuables and become Christians. If not, they would die. They refused to renounce their faith and with no alternative, they chose to die - at their own hands. So, fathers took the lives of their children then their wives, then they murdered each other. In the end, it is understood, only two remained, the leader of the community, Joseph of York and the Rabbi, Yomtob. The Rabbi intoned prayers over the remains of his slaughtered community and then, after taking the life of Joseph, he took his own: taking the sin of suicide upon himself.

The next morning the few Jews who remained, believing that they could trust the rebels to keep their words, opened the gates. The rebels stormed in, murdered the Jews and finding that they had set light to all their valuable goods, left the castle to burn to the ground.

In 1245, Henry III ordered that the castle be rebuilt, but a short time after its completion the walls suddenly turned bright red. The people of York were descended from the rebels in 1190 and had something on their consciences; they believed that the stones of the castle were running with the blood of the Jews.

Jews shunned the city for centuries and it was not until the time of the Commonwealth in the middle of the seventeenth century that the Lord Protector, Oliver Cromwell, invited Jews to return to York to live. Since that time a Jewish community has lived in York and in 1980 they formally forgave the City for that atrocity in 1190. These two events might explain why the phenomenon of the walls turning red has not re-occurred. However, close examination of Clifford's Tower will show that even today, some parts have a pale red tint to them. A sad reminder of a horrible part of the City's history.

This incident might stand as an ancient curiosity if it weren't for some recent experiments carried out by Arnall Bloxham in the 1950's and 60's. Under hypnosis his subjects were able to "travel" back in time, to other "lives" they have apparently lived in history. These regressions were recorded and later many investigated by Jeffery Iverson and published in his book *More Lives Than One?* Jane Evans was one of Bloxham's subjects and she regressed to twelfth century York where she said she was a Jewess whose name was Rebecca. Under hypnosis, she described life for Jews in the city and the start of the uprising. Fearing for her life, she had gone, with her family, to the castle but when they got there they found that the gates were already closed and they were unable to get in. They ran to hide in the nearest church where they took refuge in the crypt, hoping that they would not be found by their persecutors. But they hoped in vain, their persecutors searched the church, found them in the crypt and horribly slaughtered them.

In each of the regressions where Jane Evans reached the point of Rebecca's death, the last words she always uttered were, "Dark ... dark."

At the time of the regression Jane Evans was in her thirties, she had only a limited knowledge of English history and had never been to York; yet under hypnosis she could describe twelfth century York in great detail. Her regressions were filmed and tape recorded and when the tapes were played to Professor Barrie Dobson of York University, an acknowledged expert on the massacre of the Jews in 1190, he was very impressed with the detail she could give of her "life" at that time. Especially as most of the information should really have been known by only the most learned of historians. But one element of her story caused concern - her description of the church where she ran away to hide. She said it was the nearest church and once inside they hid in the crypt. In York there is only one church that has a crypt, the Minster, and in one regression, she stated quite definitely that is was not the Minster where she ran away to hide.

St Mary's in Castlegate, is the nearest church to the castle and, although built later than 1190, it is in the location she described and was, therefore, the first church examined by researchers, but it had no crypt. So, on the basis of this fundamental inaccuracy, her regression could not be accepted as a credible proof for reincarnation.

Some years later, in 1975, St Mary's was desanctified and converted into a museum. During the renovation a workman accidentally demolished a part of a wall and discovered a crypt under the chancel. The description matched that of a Norman church that may have stood on there before St Mary's was built. This was confirmed later by discoveries of re-used Roman or Anglo-Saxon stonework below the present floor level of the church. Positive proof that there was an older church on the site at the time when Rebecca said she took refuge there.

A church with a crypt.

... Churches

Churches seem to attract a large number of ghosts, but rarely is there information about their identity nor an explanation for their appearances. One reason for this might be that the church is the place we go to for private consolation while we are alive and if we continue to do so when we are dead, our anonymity is assured.

York has lost many of its churches over the centuries, some remain as buildings but are now used as tea-rooms, community centres or museums, others have gone altogether. But one remains, as it were, as a ghost. At the bottom of Shambles once stood St Crux, a fine fifteenth century church which was demolished in 1886. A public outcry caused the authorities to alter their plans for wholesale redevelopment of the area and to use the stone from the church to build a small parish room on the site containing a few relics as a pale reminder of the church that was once there. Added to the loss of the church is the loss of its ghosts.

People passing St Crux in the early hours of the morning often saw a man inside looking out into the street. He was seen, most frequently, by women cleaners on their way to work in those quiet moments between dawn and day. Although the women were bold enough to call out to him, they never dared to go into the church; something in his appearance forbade them to enter and, perhaps to their relief, he never came out. So, his identity and the reason he was there, if, in fact, he was there, will remain a mystery.

In days gone by, a watch was kept on the night-time city by the York Waits. During the winter months, dressed in their scarlet coats, they performed a civic duty by processing through the streets to call out the time, act as night watchmen and give a forecast of the weather. But most important was their music, popular tunes of the day played on shawms, viols, hurdy-gurdies and bombards.

Usually they were the only ones abroad; most people wisely being in their beds, but as they passed St Crux their number was mysteriously increased by a young woman who would appear from the graveyard. She was described as very beautiful and dressed in white. She would follow a little behind the Waits and stop whenever they did. As they played their music she stood in rapture as if in another world, then followed when they moved on. At first the players were disturbed by the appearance of this

woman who enacted the same ritual every night without variation. Soon they became accustomed to her being there, sometimes they would call to her to join them, but she never responded and never came close enough to speak to them; she just followed and listened. She stayed with them until they reached the top of Shambles, then as they turned into Goodramgate, she simply disappeared.

Some ghosts appear on several occasions to the same or different people, but sometimes a haunting happens only once. Like the night when a police constable passing St Crux was drawn to the sound of the organ being played in the church. He drew closer to be able to hear more clearly. Light seeped from under the door and the sound of the organ was booming louder and deeper in a mournful recital of the Funeral March. He was surprised that a funeral was taking place at that time of night and looking around he was amazed by the absence of a hearse and mourners' carriages. Something was not right and he grew suspicious. Cautiously he moved towards the door, but drew back as the sound of the organ fell to a whisper and the door slowly opened.

As light spilled into the street the atmosphere turned unnaturally cold. He stood there awe-struck as he sensed the space around him being filled with people, his eyes told him he was alone, but he could hear the rustling of dresses and felt people brushing against him as he stood in their way at the door of the church. He mind was in turmoil, blood rushed to his brain and he felt his control of the situation slipping away. He was surrounded by people who could touch him and make sounds that he could hear, but he couldn't see anyone. Just when he thought his mind was going completely, the atmosphere began to return to normal, the door of the church slowly closed, the light faded within and music stopped. Suddenly he was alone, bewildered and frightened in the cold, dark street.

Fearing for his sanity, he told the story to just one trusted colleague. Much later it was passed on to Elliot O'Donnell who recorded it in his book *Haunted Churches*, but the event never appeared in any police records.

Not far from where St Crux once stood is St Saviour's, although it too is no longer a church. Beside it at one time was a family mansion which, for reasons no longer known, fell into disuse. It was believed that some tragedy within the family had caused them to desert the house leaving a spiritual legacy that prevented them from ever returning to their ancestral home.

There is no record of the nature of that tragedy but each night as midnight struck a beautiful young woman appeared at the door of the empty and neglected house. With all the poise that came from generations of genteel breeding she walked past the church to its the door, then waited as if expecting someone to arrive at any moment. The sight of this woman waiting at the church door disturbed the locals. She would pace slowly back and forth, watching the street for someone who had promised to meet her. But then, at the stroke of one, with no-one having arrived, she slowly returned to her deserted home. Inspections of the house by daylight revealed no signs of habitation, yet every night she appeared at the door and returned to it an hour later. The house remained unsold and, as the years went by, became more forlorn and dilapidated in appearance, convincing everyone that it was haunted. Later it was demolished to make way for Lady Hewley's Hospital and with the house no longer there, the haunting stopped.

This appears to give some support to the theory that whenever a location is changed, either by building on it, or altering the building that is there, it is possible to either start or stop a haunting. In this case it appears to have stopped one. Perhaps.

All Saints' Church, a short distance away in Pavement, is still a Parish Church but appears no longer to have its ghost. At one time whenever there was a funeral at the church, the congregation would be increased by one uninvited guest. She was described as young and very beautiful, with her long hair in ringlets or curls and she was always dressed in white; although no-one is sure whether she was wearing a wedding dress or a funeral shroud. Most think the latter.

Whenever there was a funeral service in the All Saints', she would appear at the door giving a smile of comfort to the mourners. She looked so real and natural that very few people realised that she was not, in fact, one of the bereaved. As they filed their doleful way past her into the church, they may have noticed an atmosphere of peace and harmony that she created. Then as the coffin arrived, she would follow it into the church and take a place in the pews. Probably the mourners would have been too deep in their grief to notice, that as the service began, the young woman who had welcomed them at the door, just faded into the atmosphere.

York's most beautiful ghost, as she has been described, has not been seen for some time now; perhaps because it is quite some time since there has been a funeral at All Saints' Church.

Perhaps the most poignant of these church hauntings comes from St Olave's in Marygate. Mrs Peggy Atkinson, a regular worshipper there found her attention straying from the service one Sunday. From her position in the back pew she could see all the congregation, most of whom she knew very well but on this occasion she was fascinated by two people sitting in front of her whom she had never seen before. Their clothes seemed strangely old fashioned, she thought the style was from around the time World War I. The couple, a woman and a boy, were in an obvious state of anguish, both were weeping and the woman was constantly hugging and consoling the boy. They seemed oblivious to the service in the agony of their distress.

For a few moments Mrs Atkinson forgot about them as she knelt in prayer but when she rose the couple had gone. They had made no sound nor disturbance as they went and the door beside her had made no noise. After the service she asked the verger who the couple were, but although he had been sitting in the same pew, he didn't recognise them from her description, adding that there were no strangers in the church that day.

Beside Holy Trinity Church in Micklegate stands a row of mediaeval cottages, now used as shops; at one time they adjoined the gates to Holy Trinity Priory. In mediaeval times the gates were the site for the first performances of the York Cycle of Mystery Plays. The Priory gates were demolished in 1858 to make way for the building of Priory Street, the name of which is the only indication that a priory ever stood in that part of York. In the graveyard of Holy Trinity, just inside the gate is a set of stocks; close inspection reveals a conundrum - they have only five holes, it's a puzzle how many people they were able to accommodate. Another unusual aspect is contained on the notice fixed to the gate. The last sentence advises of an historic haunting of the church.

The story was told by S. Baring Gould in his *Yorkshire Oddities* in which he included correspondence from people who claimed to have seen several ghosts at a time. Before Holy Trinity was altered in the 1880's, there was a gallery at the west end of the church and it was from there that the ghosts were seen. One account tells of a figure appearing in the glass of the east window, directly opposite the gallery, "a graceful figure of a girl of eighteen or twenty years crossed the outside of the stained east window with a light, free step. She was entirely covered with a fine lace veil which, as she walked and met the air showed the outline of the head and figure ... Two or three other figures also appear but I never thought them as distinct as the first." However, another witness was more definite about the other figures. "Of the three figures two were evidently those of women, and the third was a little child. The two women were very distinct in appearance. One was tall and very graceful, and the other middle-sized; we called the second one the nursemaid."

These figures were seen on a number of occasions by various people, but the format was generally the same. First the young woman would appear in the glass of the east window and move across it, half way across she would stop and wave, this gesture would cause the appearance of the older woman and the child. "Both figures then bent over the child, and seemed to bemoan its fate."

There was a great deal of speculation concerning the identities of these people and the significance of the dates of their appearances. Some tried to associate the appearances with Trinity Sunday; but sightings were reported all through the year. Others tried to find logical explanations and suggested the cause was sunlight reflected from a nearby window and yet the figures were seen on dull days as well as bright. One theory was that the people were outside the window and could be seen through it, but at the time of the sightings there was a high wall just outside the east end of the church, so it was impossible for anyone to stand outside the church and still be seen.

Among the explanations seemed to demonstrate that these figures could, in fact, have been ghosts. It was the story of a young family who lived in the Bishophill area of York in the first half of the nineteenth century. The father died tragically young and was buried at the east end of Holy Trinity Church, leaving his grieving wife with only their infant daughter, a living memory of her husband. But to add to her grief, her daughter was taken from her by one of the frequent outbreaks of typhus, typhoid and cholera that occurred at that time. Plague regulations prevented the child from being buried in the churchyard, and her body had to be carried to the plague pit outside the City walls.

This was all too much for the mother who lost her will to live. When she died a little time later she was laid bedside her husband in Holy Trinity graveyard; but was unable to rest easy in her grave. Her ghost would rise and seek the only member of her family who was missing, her daughter. She searched among the tombstones until the nurse brought the ghost of the child from the other side of the walls to be with her mother for a brief while before once again being separated for eternity.

The identity of the nurse is a mystery; she may have actually been the child's nurse carried off by the plague at the same time and buried with her. Or she may be another ghost that has been seen in the area called "the grey lady of Priory Street". She may have been connected with the Priory that was dissolved by the troops of Henry VIII during the Reformation. Some people have suggested that she may be Prioress who acts as a nurse or carer in the Holy Trinity Church haunting.

These ghosts have not been seen since 1886 when the gallery was removed and the new chancel was added over that part of the graveyard where the parents were buried. Possibly incorporating the unquiet grave into the church has given it everlasting peace.

But that is not, perhaps the last of the hauntings of Holy Trinity. Not long ago a woman visiting the city at the time of the Early Music Festival, wandered into the church and sat quietly for a time listening to some beautiful music from the organ. Thinking that she had inadvertently walked into a rehearsal for one of the concerts she sat very quietly and enjoyed her private preview. When the recital finished she went to congratulate the performer. Her blood ran cold when she found no-one there, the organ locked and herself alone in the church.

... The Dancing School

The Bishophill area of York has played a long role in the City's history. In Roman times it was the Colonia, the self-governing, civil part of Eboracum. There, up until the beginning of the fourth century, pagan gods were worshipped in temples dedicated to Serapis and Mithras. Later, at the end of the Viking era, Eric Bloodaxe in flight from his enemies, took refuge in the church on the site of St Mary's, Bishophill Junior and during the Dissolution of the Monasteries, Holy Trinity Priory was dissolved under the orders of Henry VIII. With such a history, it is not altogether surprising that people have experienced strange and unexplained occurrences and sensed uneasy feelings in the area.

One place of unusual activity in Bishophill is the dancing school run by Rita and Dennis Cole in a building adjoining St Mary's, Bishophill

Junior. A large number of strange and unexplained events have occurred there over the years; people have witnessed objects moving on their own, there have been inexplicable sounds and cold spots, mysterious foot steps and sightings of people who were long dead. Of these stories, there some that deserve to be told in detail.

One incident was witnessed on several occasions by as many as five people. During a class, the dancing had stopped for a while when the atmosphere in the room suddenly turned icy cold and in the silence that followed, footsteps were heard crossing from the side of the building nearest to the church to the centre of the dance floor. They stopped. Then there was the sound of money being poured from a box onto a heavy wooden table. And then, as if being counted, the money was slid coin by coin across the table and back into the box. As this process continued the volume of the sound increased until at last it was concluded by an ear-shattering crash as the lid of the box was slammed shut. The footsteps then returned the way they had come and as they faded away the atmosphere in the room slowly returned to normal; although the witnesses never did.

At other times there has been a violent knocking on the rear doors to the school. One time a man, alone in the building shouted out, "Come round the front, the doors are always open." He was ignored and the violence of the knocking increased. The handle was being turned and the door was shaken with such force that he became alarmed for the safety of the person outside. He ran to the door and shouted through it, "Run round the front, the door's open, this one's locked and I can't find the key."

Again he was ignored and the violence of the knocking increased. Aware that his voice might not be heard above the sound of the banging, he moved a table to the door and stood on it so that he could look through the window above it to indicate to whoever was outside that they should run round to the front. As he did so, he was shocked and surprised to find that there was no one outside, but the door was still being knocked and shaken.

Another time when Mr and Mrs Cole were away taking their annual holiday, a colleague was looking after the school. He was one of the many sceptics who had heard of the hauntings but did not believe in any of them. One night when the dancing had finished and everyone had gone home, he was switching off the lights and locking up before going home himself. He was just about to leave the building, he turned for one final check that everything was in order and noticed something odd. At the far end of the hall a book was sliding from the shelf. It was moving horizontally with almost hypnotic speed, away from the shelf to a position in mid air three or four feet away, where it hung suspended for a short while before falling to the floor with such a force that the tremendous thump it created seemed to resonate in his head for ages.

He left the building that night in such a hurry that, later on, the police had to go to the home of Mrs Cole's mother, Mrs Marshall, to ask her if she would kindly return to the dancing school with them to switch off the lights and lock the door.

Mrs Marshall, herself, was not immune to strange and unusual activities in the building. She frequently helped out at the school and one day was working alone in the cellar when the atmosphere suddenly turned unnaturally cold and oppressively musty. It then became hostile; so much so, that without being told, she knew her presence wasn't wanted. She immediately turned and started to leave, but she hadn't gone more than a couple of paces when she was violently pushed across the cellar floor ending in a heap on the steps. She thought that it was a member of the dancing school who had hidden down there and was playing a joke on her, so she turned round to tell them what she thought of them; only to find that the room was still empty, but the feeling of hostility was now so powerful that the only thing she could do was to scramble up the steps and vow never to return there again.

Some people tried to investigate these occurrences and record their findings. In a way they were to be disappointed because none of the previously reported incidents happened while they were there, but what did happen has added to the list of stories to be told. They noticed that a small area in the centre of the room was colder than everywhere else, but there was no obvious reason for it. This was followed by a sequence of electrical faults, firstly a power socket failed, then a recorder motor seized and when these were repaired, the microphone wouldn't work. They sent for a replacement, insisting that it should be thoroughly tested before it was brought into the building. That was done, but once inside, it failed to work.

Some years later a BBC television crew had a similar experience, when they arrived in the hall the gas heaters refused to light and they had to work in coldness, their equipment failed to work properly and much of their work had to be re-shot in haste, forcing them to settle for less than perfect results. Minutes after they left the building the heaters functioned perfectly.

One cold March night a small group of people huddled in the porch of the dancing school, sheltering from icy rain as their guide told them the ghost stories of the building. It was dark outside and they were grateful for the light and the respite from the wind and occasional hail. Suddenly the story was interrupted by the sound of footsteps coming along the passage towards the door. On a night when ice was falling from the sky, their blood ran cold.

A few seconds later the immediate fear was relieved as Rita Cole turned the corner and walked towards them. She listened patiently for a while and confirmed all the stories the guide told. Then looking out into the street, she told them that she was on her way to give a demonstration of dancing, but as her taxi had not arrived she would tell them a story.

One night a dancer came into the class looking a little flustered. She walked straight up to Mrs Cole and said, "Who was that woman who just went out?"

Mrs Cole replied, "I don't know, I didn't see anyone leave. What did she look like?"

She described the woman but said that what worried her was the look on her face, "It was as if she was looking straight through me," she said.

"Would you recognise her if you saw her again?" Mrs Cole asked.

"Oh yes," she replied, "I'll never forget that face."

Mrs Cole went into the office and brought out a photograph. On it were people attending a dinner for dance teachers.

"Is she there?" asked Mrs Cole.

The woman looked at the photograph for a couple of seconds; there were about fifty faces on it. "That's her!" she said pointing to one of them.

"That's Mary MacPherson," said Mrs Cole. "She started the dancing school and it still bears her name. Sadly, she's been dead many years now, but its nice to know she is still interested in the school."

The taxi arrived and with a wistful smile bade the Ghost Walkers goodnight and slipped into the night.

... Scrivener

At the turn of the twentieth century John Scrivener owned an old house not far from the River Ouse which he used to let out to small businesses that would rent a room or two from him. Every night, his house-keeper would go there to tidy up, ready for the next day's business, but very often she had to leave her work undone and go home early, because she said, there was an atmosphere in the house that frightened her and she heard noises that terrified her. She heard thumps, she heard rumblings, she heard footsteps and she heard screams. Scrivener, who was a man of his time, a product of the industrial revolution told her that everything in heaven and earth could be explained by scientific investigation. He said it was probably the sounds of an old house, settling down after the day's business and the product of her own mind. He reassured her that she could safely work in the house without fearing for her life.

She was not very satisfied with this as an explanation, but did, however, continue to work for him. A few weeks later, one evening in January, Scrivener found her stumbling down the street away from the house, she appeared to be terrified. He caught up with her and asked her what was wrong.

"Oh, sir," she said, "I can't ever go in that house again. There's such an atmosphere there. And the noises. There is such a thumping and the poor person upstairs is screaming their life away."

Scrivener could see that she wasn't going to be able to do any more work that night, so he took her home, settled her indoors and returned to the house to investigate. When he reached it he found the door was still open as she had left it in her flight and a light was burning in the hall. He let himself in, shut the door, locked it and bolted it. Then he stood in the hall for a while just to listen to the sounds of the house. As he'd expected, it was completely silent. He went into each of the downstairs rooms, intending to make a thorough investigation of the house; but every room was empty, every room was silent. Once more back in the hall, with his ears now accustomed to the silence in the house, he stood for a while to listen to the farther reaches.

It was just then, from a long way off, far above him upstairs, he heard a thump followed by a scream. This somewhat unnerved Scrivener; he hadn't expected to hear anything at all, but to hear precisely what his housekeeper had described, terrified him. But he reminded himself that he was a man of science, a man of reason and he was determined to discover what was causing this. He found a candle, lit it and slowly started to climb the stairs towards the sounds. As he did so his ears became more attuned to them, the thumps became more violent and the screams more terrifying. The dark house was otherwise silent and the thumps and screams seemed to resound in his head.

    On the first floor, as much to bolster his failing courage as to carry out a thorough investigation, he went into each of the rooms. But every room was empty, every room was silent. By this time he knew which room the sounds were coming from. It was the little room at the top of the house, the room that no-one ever wanted the room he'd never been able to let.

    Slowly he climbed the narrow flight of stairs that lead to the top floor, but there again he checked every room first, until at last he had no choice but to make his way down the corridor to the attic room at the end. He unlocked the door, threw it open wide and thrust his candle inside to break the darkness.

Inside, apart from a cloying, musty smell the room was completely empty. Opposite him there was a window where the ceiling sloped down to meet the floor and beside the window was a door that lead to a cupboard. From behind that door came the thumps followed by the screams.

Scrivener crossed the uneven floor, put his candle down on the window sill, opened the door and stepped back. Inside, high up by the ceiling was a water tank, a ball floated on top of the water and, occasionally, it thumped against the side of the tank releasing water down the pipes that had recently been frozen in the cold weather, but the rapid thaw that followed caused an airlock and as the water passed the airlock, it screamed. Scrivener stood back satisfied, he'd known all along that he was right and he looked forward to the next day when he would bring his housekeeper into the room to show her that it was as he had said, the sounds of an old house and the product of her own imagination.

At that moment his candle went out.

He stood in the total darkness, alarmed and terrified, he fumbled to strike another light and held it towards the candle, only to find that it had simply burned away. Another logical explanation. Relieved, he turned round and held up the light to find the door and make his way out of the building. As the flame burned to his fingertips he extinguished it and dropped the match to the floor. It was then that he heard, along way off, far below him in the cellar, the rumble of bricks being thrown onto a stone-flag floor.

At the same instant the atmosphere turned icy cold and tingles of fear ran up and down Scrivener's spine. He stood there, paralysed with fear as that sound was followed by the sound of footsteps laboriously climbing the stairs towards him. At first he thought it was one of his tenants who had forgotten something and had returned to their office to collect it. But he remembered that he'd not only locked the door, he'd bolted it as well. He was alone in the house, but someone was climbing the stairs towards him.

Unable to move, he realised that the only way for him to escape was to run towards the sounds and as he listened he was able to identify two strange, but distinct qualities about them. The first was the sound of leather boots on bare, wooden stairs, yet Scrivener knew that the stairs were carpeted. And the other was on every second tread, a faint metallic jangle.

On the first landing the footsteps didn't stop but continued up the narrow flight of stairs that led to the floor that he was on. When they reached it, they turned and moved down the corridor towards the attic room. Soon he was able to see a silver-grey shape occupying the doorway, it didn't stop, but moved straight towards him. His eyes bulged, his mouth gaped but he was unable to move or make a sound, he just stood there and awaited his fate.

A few seconds later the figure stopped, silent, in front of him; then, after a while, it moved on beyond Scrivener, through the window at his side, falling to the ground with a terrifying scream. A scream that was matched only by Scrivener's own as he ran from the building.

He never entered the building again.

Sometime later, builders working in the cellar, had to remove several flag stones from the floor. Underneath they found the remains of a man; a large man, a military man. On the remains of his face was the look of one who had died in extreme terror or agony, on his body the shreds of a military uniform and on his feet were leather riding boots, attached to which were metal spurs, one of them was broken and every time it was moved ... it jangled.

... Treasurer's House

It was 22nd February, 1953 and if anyone had asked Harry Martindale before that date what he thought about ghosts, he would probably have replied, very little. It wasn't a subject uppermost in the eighteen year-old apprentice plumber's mind; on balance, he might have admitted, that he didn't believe in them. The 22nd February, 1953 was to change his mind and his life for ever.

It had started much as any day; that morning Harry had made his way down the cold, dark cobbled streets behind York Minster to the Treasurer's House. Once inside he carried his bag of tools into the basement and then down the narrow tunnel that led to what had been the garden cellar when Frank Green owned the house at the turn of the century. Harry's job was to help to convert the cellar into a boiler room, he had already been working down there for over a week and was quite happy to be left to his own devices. He leaned his short ladder against the wall and, in the poor light provided by the single electric light bulb, started work on the hole he was making in the vaulted brick roof of the tiny room.

After a while he became aware of a musical note which appeared to be coming from the wall against which he was working. It sounded like a trumpet, but was ugly, discordant. At first he thought little of it, but as time went by the sound appeared to be getting louder; or perhaps, nearer, because a few moments later, a Roman soldier stepped through the wall where Harry was working.

In shock and amazement, Harry fell from his ladder and scrambled across the earth floor to the corner of the room where he attempted to hide as that soldier was followed by another. This one mounted on the back of a great, untidy cart horse, he was slumped across its neck and appeared to be fast asleep. They were followed by a troop of soldiers. Harry was too frightened to think of counting them, but guessed that there were more than twenty. They appeared in two's through the wall against which he had been working, crossed the cellar floor and disappeared through the wall on the other side of the cellar.

Suddenly it seemed as if Harry was in another world; he had the feeling that his world, only a few feet above his head, no longer existed. He was in a new place that hadn't been there two minutes before which was populated by people just an arm's length away, who appeared to be totally unaware of his presence. The soldiers were so near and looked so real that he felt that if he reached out he could touch them, but the only thought on his mind, however, was if he could see them, so close and so clearly, one of them had only to turn a head to see him, and then what would happen? So he didn't move nor make a sound, but he watched and it was to his relief that none of them turned to look in his direction. Slowly the details of the way they looked started to fill his mind. The first thing he noticed about these soldiers was that they were very short. They looked exhausted, disorderly and dejected. Their clothes were untidy and not at all like the Roman Army uniform seen in history books or films. They wore badly made kilts that were patchily dyed green. Broad bands of leather were brought about their chests to form jerkins, some carried round shields and they all wore short swords on the right hand side. They had long, fair hair and beards that were ginger and they muttered to each other but in no language that Harry had ever heard. It certainly wasn't Latin nor vernacular Italian. The trumpet one soldier was blowing was long and battered and its ugly sound pierced Harry's ears.

Very little of this, Harry admitted later, resembled the usual description of a Roman army. But what made him think that these were Roman soldiers were their helmets; the only part of their uniform that was consistent throughout the whole troop and the only thing he seemed to remember from his limited knowledge of Roman history. The large metal chin-straps, the polished metal domes and the brightly coloured plumes; had it not been for this, he would not have thought that these were Roman soldiers at all.

But one image locked itself firmly in Harry's mind; as these men made their bedraggled way across the cellar floor, they weren't marching across, they appeared to be walking on their knees. He could see nothing of them below their knees.

When the last of the soldiers disappeared through the wall, Harry dashed from the cellar and scrambled up the stairs to the real world. At the top of the stairs a dark, looming figure, framed against the light of a window, barred his way. Harry shrank back in fear. The figure spoke, "You've just seen the soldiers, haven't you?" With relief, Harry recognised the Curator and slowly told his story.

Later, he was interviewed by experts in Roman history who were more impressed by the things that Harry didn't say than by what he did. His description of the soldiers didn't match the popular image gained from Hollywood films and they didn't sound like an army that had conquered most of Northern Europe, they were tired and scruffy. But, surprisingly, the experts felt that he had described the soldiers correctly, they sounded like soldiers from the later part of the Roman era, between 380 AD, when the Empire was breaking up and 410 AD, when they left Britain to fend for itself. The soldiers that Harry saw were probably Auxiliaries, recruited from among the Brigantes, the celtic tribes-people who lived in Eboracum before the Romans came. This may explain why the soldiers lacked enthusiasm, wore their own clothes, had fair hair and ginger beards and why he had never heard their language before. It was probably old Gaelic.

And some of the things that Harry didn't know also fascinated them. He hadn't known that nearly two thousand years ago, the place where he was working was the Roman fortress and, although he had described the trumpet with its ugly sound, he was totally unaware of any significance. The trumpet was used by the troops as a signal that they were friendly forces approaching the gates of a Roman fortress. Exactly what Roman soldiers would be doing as they approached the Principia, the headquarters of the Roman Fortress.

But the most amazing piece of evidence was to come a short time later, the cellar where he had been working was the subject of an archaeological dig and beneath its floor they found a Roman road, the Via Decumana, leading from the Principia, the Headquarters of the fortress, to the north east gate, the Porta Decumana.

So what Harry saw wasn't an army marching on its knees, but the ghosts of Roman soldiers marching on a road that was buried beneath the cellar floor.

Bibliography

BARING-GOULD, S. (1890) Yorkshire oddities and incidents. London: Condon, Methuen.
BOOTH, R. K. (1990) York: the history and heritage of a city: London: Barrie & Jenkins.
BROCKBANK, J. L. and HOLMES W. M. (1909) York in English history. London: A. Brown & Sons.
BROOKESMITH, Peter (ed) (1984) Great hauntingss. London: Orbis.
BUTLER, R. M. (1974) The bars and walls of York: a handbook for visitors. York: Architectural and York Archaeological Society.
BUTTERY, Darrell The vanished buildings of York.
HALL, Jenny and JONES, Christine (1992) Roman Britain. London: BBC Educational Publishing.
IVERSON, Jefferey (1976) More lives than one? London: Souvenir Press.
JONES, Mark W. (1983) A walk around the snickleways of York. York: William Sessions.
MITCHELL, John V. Ghosts of an ancient city. York: Cerialis Press.
NEWMAN, P. R. The royal castle of York. York: York Castle Museum.
O'DONNELL, Elliott (1939) Haunted churches. London: Quality Press.
PALLISER, D. M. (1990) Borthwick Papers No. 70 Domesday York. York: University of York.
PALLISER, David & PALLISER, Mary (1979) York as they saw it - from Alcuin to Lord Esher. York: William Sessions.
PEACOCK, A J, Theatre Royal York. York: York Educational Settlement.
PRESSLEY, I. P. A York miscellany. London: A Brown & Sons.
RANDLES, Jenny and HOUGH, Peter (1993) The afterlife: an investigation into the the mysteries of life after death. London: BCA.
ROYAL COMMISSION ON HISTORICAL MONUMENTS (1981) York: historic buildings in the central area. London: HMSO.
STACPOOLE, Alberic (ed) (1972) The noble city of York. York: Cerialis Press.
YORKSHIRE EVENING PRESS, Various authors. News and features articles. York: York and County Press.
YORKSHIRE MUSEUM (1985) Roman life: at the Yorkshire Museum. York: The Yorkshire Museum.